Channel Islands National Park

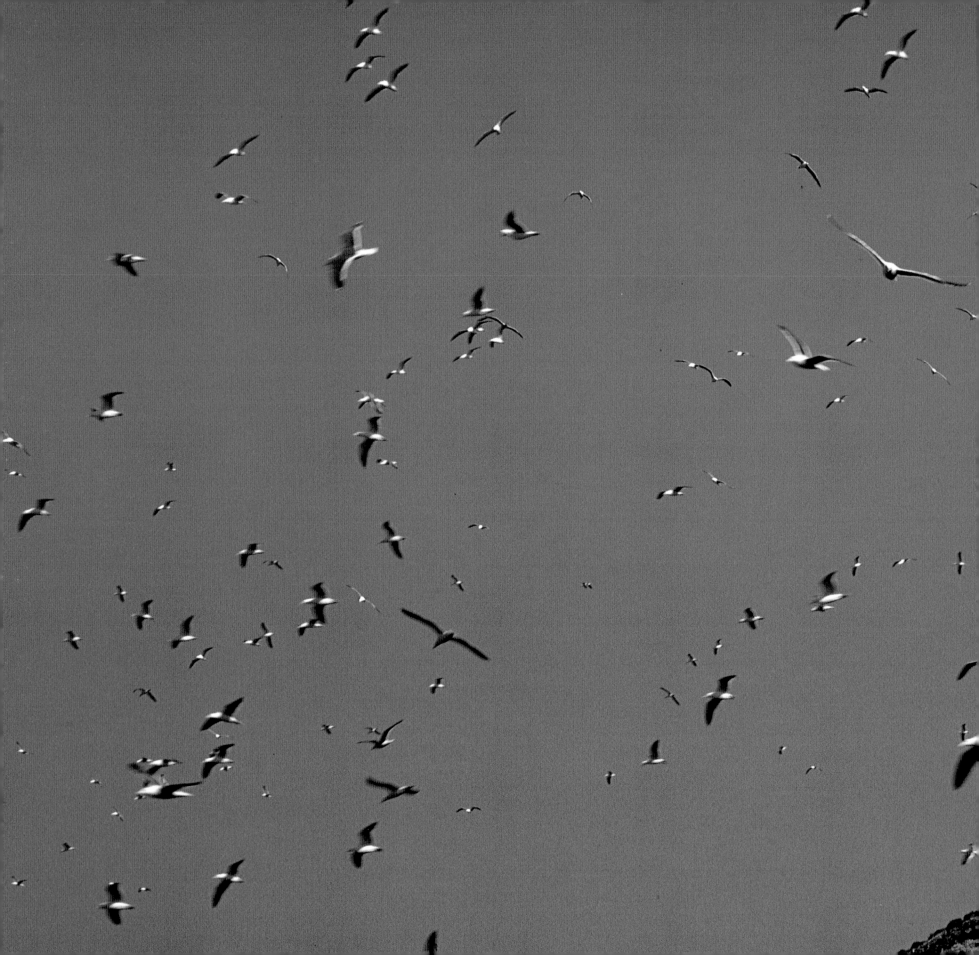

CHANNNEL ISLANDS NATIONAL PARK

A
PHOTOGRAPHIC
INTERPRETATION
BY
TIM HAUF

Channel Islands National Park
A Photographic Interpretation by Tim Hauf

Published by Tim Hauf Photography

Photography by Tim Hauf

Book design by Peggy Ferris Design

Text by Cynthia Anderson

ISBN 1-885324-11-1
First Printing August 1996
Second Printing September 1999
Third Printing January 2003
Printed and bound in Hong Kong

Above: Bechers Bay, Santa Rosa Island.
Opposite above: Northern elephant seals and sea rocket.

Acknowledgements

Publishing a book of this type requires the involvement of many dedicated and enthusiastic people and organizations in order to obtain the photos, properly identify the subjects, and verify the accuracy of the information presented.
Sincere thanks to the following for their assistance and support:

Channel Islands National Park and its employees.

The Nature Conservancy–Santa Cruz Island Preserve.

William Ehorn, Superintendent Channel Islands National Monument 1974-1980, Channel Islands National Park 1980-1989, for writing the foreword.

Steve Junak, Herbarium Curator of the Santa Barbara Botanical Garden, for invaluable assistance in plant identification.

John Johnson Ph.D., of the Santa Barbara Museum of Natural History, for providing information regarding the Chumash presence on the Channel Islands.

The Department of Recreation and Leisure Studies at California State University, Long Beach, for providing a unique insight into the natural history of the islands.

Marla Daily, President of the Santa Cruz Island Foundation.

Previous pages: Lighthouse, Anacapa Island.
Above: The Californian approaches Arch Rock, Anacapa Island.

CONTENTS

Foreword

BY BILL EHORN

The highlight of my career with the National Park Service was the opportunity to be instrumental in establishing Channel Islands National Park. During the fifteen years I spent there (1974-1989) I proudly referred to it as the "World's Greatest National Park." I never tired of spending time on the islands and was constantly amazed by their outstanding natural and cultural resources of world significance.

On clear days, the five Channel Islands of the park—Santa Barbara, Anacapa, Santa Cruz, Santa Rosa, and San Miguel—as well as the three southern Channel Islands outside it, are visible from vantage points along the Southern California coastline from San Diego to Point Conception. While the islands received their first European visitor, Juan Rodríguez Cabrillo, in 1542, they are little known to the nearly 20 million people who live within 100 miles of their shores. Buffered by the great Pacific Ocean wilderness, they remain mysterious and only lightly visited.

The Channel Islands were evaluated and considered for National Park status as early as 1932. While the islands did indeed meet the criteria to be set aside as a national park, their isolation as well as the more pressing needs of other areas combined to delay further consideration.

In August 1938, Channel Islands National Monument, consisting of Anacapa and Santa Barbara islands, was established by President Franklin Roosevelt to preserve prehistoric remains of mammoth dwarf elephants and other scientific features. Ironically, the remains of the dwarf elephants, while found on four of the Channel Islands, were not present on the islands within the monument.

Through a cooperative agreement between the Secretaries of the Navy and the Interior, the National Park Service assumed management of San Miguel Island in 1976. This allowed the National Park Service to control visitation and protect the islands' resources. In 1978, Dr. Carey Stanton, the owner of 54,000 acres on Santa Cruz Island (approximately 90 percent of the island) sold his land to The Nature Conservancy, which has policies closely aligned with those of the National Park Service.

After the acquisition of the Stanton property by The Nature Conservancy, it seemed to make sense to push ahead with the establishment of a national park. Congressman Robert Lagomarsino initiated the legislation. At first he was concerned that national park status would draw too much attention to the islands, attracting more people than they could accommodate. The legislation incorporated wording to restrict visitor use and to authorize an inventory of terrestrial and mammal species to better protect the park's natural resources.

On March 5, 1980, President Jimmy Carter signed the bill that established Channel Islands National Park as America's fortieth national park. The legislation provided for the acquisition of Santa Rosa Island and the east end of Santa Cruz Island, and directed the Park Service to cooperate with The Nature Conservancy in management of their portion of Santa Cruz Island. Since then, Santa Rosa Island was purchased in December 1986. Portions of the east end of Santa Cruz Island were acquired in 1990, 1991 and 1997.

Early on it was recognized that the marine resources surrounding the islands must be managed in concert with the terrestrial resources. In September 1980, Channel Islands National Marine Sanctuary was established to provide a buffer around the islands and increase their protection.

I am grateful for the wonderful time I spent on the islands and the many memories I have of them prior to the establishment of the park—and also for the opportunity to help preserve and protect the islands for future generations. In my mind Channel Islands National Park remains the "Greatest National Park in the World."

William H. Ehorn,
Former Superintendent
Channel Islands National Monument, 1974-1980
Channel Islands National Park, 1980-1989

Opposite: Freshwater marsh, Santa Rosa Island.

The Islands

The stark beauty and rich resources of California's Channel Islands have long attracted and fascinated visitors. Hundreds of miles of unspoiled coastline provide secluded habitats for breeding colonies of pinnipeds (seals and sea lions) and sea birds, including the California brown pelican and western gulls. Many plants and animals found on the islands are endemic, occurring nowhere else on earth.

Altogether, the Channel Islands span a distance of 160 miles from Point Conception to San Diego, and lie between 11 and 60 miles offshore. They comprise two distinct groups: four Northern islands (San Miguel, Santa Rosa, Santa Cruz, and Anacapa) and four Southern islands (Santa Barbara, Santa Catalina, San Nicolas, and San Clemente). All four of the Northern islands are part of Channel Islands National Park, while just one of the Southern group, Santa Barbara Island, belongs to the park.

The islands received their name from the deep ocean channels that separate them from the mainland and from each other. They are classified as "fringing islands" because of their placement along the edge of the North American continent. The complex sea bed between the Channel Islands and the mainland, known as the Continental Borderland, is filled with sea mounts, basins, escarpments, and submarine canyons. Portions of this borderland date back as much as 100 million years.

The islands themselves were formed by a combination of volcanic activity, changing sea levels, and plate tectonics. Volcanic activity, including lava flows and ash falls, erupted throughout the region between 24-10 million years ago (Miocene period). Simultaneously, the Western Transverse Ranges, which lie south of the Santa Barbara Channel, began their clock-wise rotation—a movement which still draws the Channel Islands closer to the mainland at the rate of over six mm per year.

At the onset of the Ice Age, about 5.2 million years ago (Pliocene period), ocean levels dropped as the polar icecaps expanded and the first islands emerged. Much later, as the icecaps melted and sea levels rose again, "surf-cut" marine terraces formed around the islands and the mainland coast.

This rapid sea-level rise ended about 6,000 years ago. Throughout this time, intensive tectonic activity created numerous faults; today the Channel Islands Fault Zone is a major system extending from Pasadena to west of San Miguel Island.

Scientific evidence proves that the islands were never linked to the mainland by a land bridge. It is now believed that prehistoric mammoths swam to the islands—much as their descendants, the elephants, swim today. Once isolated offshore, they evolved from a species of giants into dwarves just five feet high. The last mammoths are thought to have died out about 12,000 years ago. Their fossilized remains have been discovered on San Miguel, Santa Rosa, Santa Cruz, and San Nicolas islands.

The beginning of human settlement is generally accepted as the end of the Pleistocene, 10,000 to 12,000 years ago. The word *Canaliño,* meaning "channel people," refers to all the Channel Island native peoples. The Gabrieliño people occupied the Southern Channel Islands, and the Chumash occupied the Northern Channel Islands. Today the Chumash are regarded as one of the most complex hunting and gathering groups of North America. The word Chumash is derived from *'anchum* ("bead

Opposite: Looking west from Anacapa Island. *Above:* East Point, Santa Rosa Island.

money"), referring to the Olivella shell disc beads they manufactured. These beads became the standard medium of exchange throughout much of Southern California.

The Island Chumash developed their own dialect and culture, distinct from the Mainland Chumash. They made use of over 200 species of kelp, ocean fish, abalone, mussels, and other intertidal species, and also hunted seals, sea lions, and sea otters for meat and pelts. When whales were stranded on shore, the Chumash extracted the oil and used the gigantic bones for house frames. Thousands of middens—mounds of shell and fish fragments—occur throughout the islands, evidence of both temporary and long-term occupation.

The Chumash traveled widely in plank canoes called *tomols,* sewn with milkweed cord and caulked with *yop,* an adhesive of pine pitch and asphalt. They traded pelts, dried fish, bead money, and other items for mainland supplies such as seeds, acorns, roots, obsidian, and animal products.

Early Spanish explorers who happened upon the Channel Islands— among them, Juan Rodríguez Cabrillo, Sebastian Vizcaíno, and Gaspar de Portolá—found the Chumash living in large domed houses thatched with seagrass, with as many as 50 people to a house. "Missionization" proceeded slowly. By the early nineteenth century, disease and famine conditions beset the islanders, and most were removed to the mainland.

Above: California brown pelicans.
Opposite: Cuyler Harbor, San Miguel Island.

When Mexico gained independence from Spain in 1821, the Channel Islands became part of the new Republic of Mexico. Three islands—Santa Cruz, Santa Rosa, and Santa Catalina—were granted to private individuals. In 1848, the Treaty of Guadalupe Hidalgo ceded California (and by default, the Channel Islands) to the United States.

The process of creating Channel Islands National Park spanned over 40 years—from the establishment of Channel Islands National Monument in 1938, to the founding of the park itself in 1980. Today the park offers visitors an unprecedented opportunity to observe rare and endangered wildlife in an uncrowded, natural setting. A visit to the islands is like a journey back in time, a chance to experience California much as it looked over a century ago.

Nearly 65 plants are endemic to the Channel Islands, including island ironwood, island cherry, island oaks, manzanita, buckwheat, and live-forever. Some of the most common endemic animals are island foxes, spotted skunks, and deer mice. A bird watcher's paradise, the islands provide a home for hundreds of land and marine species. Nesting sites of the California brown pelican, Xantus' murrelet, western gulls, and others receive special protection.

Perhaps the best known mammals found on and around the islands today are the pinnipeds—California sea lions, harbor seals, Northern fur seals, and Northern elephant seals. To observe thousands of these creatures congregated at the islands' breeding sites is one of the great spectacles of the natural world.

The Channel Islands have a captivating story to tell. This book is intended to provide an overview of the vistas, the beauty, and the unexpected treasures that await visitors to Channel Islands National Park. Photographer Tim Hauf captures the essence of Anacapa, Santa Cruz, Santa Rosa, San Miguel, and Santa Barbara islands in a portrait that highlights their tremendous diversity.

Opposite: Kayaking, Anacapa Island.
Above: Snorkeling, Santa Barbara Island.

CHAPTER ONE

Anacapa Island

In the Chumash language, *Anyapak* means "mirage" or "ever-changing"—an apt description of Anacapa Island's appearance from the mainland through fog and mist. Today the sound of the foghorn greets visitors to this tiny island, whose steep cliffs ascend over 150 feet from the crashing surf to the rolling tableland above. Though it lies just 11 miles offshore, Anacapa Island is truly a world apart.

Juan Rodríguez Cabrillo sailed past in 1542, but neither he nor any other Spanish explorer reported signs of habitation. Due to the shortage of fresh water, the Chumash occupied Anacapa Island seasonally rather than in permanent settlements. Archeologists have identified many midden sites, some of which can be visited today.

The first lighthouse was built on Anacapa in the early 1900s. Between 1902 and 1937 four different parties leased the island, the most notable being H. Bay Webster, who raised sheep and ran a fishing concession. In 1938 President Franklin Roosevelt bestowed National Monument status upon Anacapa and Santa Barbara islands. In 1970 Anacapa Island came under the jurisdiction of the National Park Service.

The three small islets that make up Anacapa Island—known as East, Middle, and West Anacapa—are inaccessible from one another except at the lowest tides. Taken together, their area covers just 1.1 square miles, making Anacapa the second smallest of the Channel Islands. Each of the islets displays its own unique characteristics.

At first glance East Anacapa appears to be an inaccessible mesa; however, it is the one of the most visited spots on the Channel Islands. From the dock at Landing Cove, 154 steps climb to the top of the island. The fog signal and lighthouse are located here. A hiking trail leads to Inspiration Point with its view along the narrow, weathered ridge of Middle Anacapa to West Anacapa and beyond to Santa Cruz Island.

Swimmers may cool off at Landing Cove on calm, summer days. Boaters often drop anchor at nearby Cathedral Cove, which is surrounded by unusual rock formations of volcanic origin. Cathedral Cave, a large, multi-chambered sea cave, can be entered by skiff or kayak. Just beyond East Anacapa, sea erosion has carved Arch Rock, a 40-foot high natural arch that is a famous local landmark.

Middle Anacapa, three miles long yet seldom more than an eighth of a mile wide, is best known as the site of a famous shipwreck. The paddlewheel steamer *Winfield Scott* grounded and sank here in 1853, and its remains can be explored by snorkelers and divers today. Fishermen formerly made their home at East Fish Camp, while to the northwest Sheep Camp served as headquarters of H. Bay Webster's operation. Because of this islet's fragile ecology, visitation is restricted.

West Anacapa, the largest of the three islets, also has the greatest topographic diversity. At 930 feet, Summit Peak forms the highest point on Anacapa Island. The beach at Frenchy's Cove is popular with visitors; this cove was named after a hermit who lived here from 1928 to 1954. At low tide, it is possible to walk from Frenchy's Cove to the south side of the island, which offers exceptional tidepools. Public access to West Anacapa is restricted to Frenchy's Cove and the tidepool area to protect the West Coast's primary nesting site for the endangered California brown pelican.

Popular snorkeling and scuba diving areas surround Anacapa Island. Divers come to see the abundant marine life in the kelp beds and explore the island's coves and sea caves. From December to April, California gray whales pass by en route from Alaska to Baja, California and back, a spectacle for all to enjoy.

Opposite: Lighthouse at sunrise.

Impressive displays of wildflowers cover East Anacapa Island following winter rains.
Opposite: The current lighthouse, built in 1932, became fully automated in 1967.

Morning dew laces a cobweb strung between the dried flowers
and dormant branches of a giant coreopsis.

Waiting for their parents to return with food, these four-week-old western gull
chicks will fledge (learn to fly) when they reach six weeks of age.

Sunset at Inspiration Point, looking toward West Anacapa Island.

One of the most awe-inspiring views in Channel Islands National Park is
this sweeping vista from Inspiration Point.

Opposite: Forests of giant bladder kelp, such as this one on the south side of
Middle Anacapa, support a diverse community of marine life.
Above: Green sea anemones and countless other marine creatures dwell
in the tidepools near Frenchy's Cove.

An ocean kayaker explores one of Anacapa's 135 charted sea caves.

Kayakers and boaters can view marine life,
including California brown pelicans and harbor seals,
at close range on the craggy rocks near Arch Rock.

Anacapa Island has many unique geological formations.
Opposite: Keyhole Rock. ***Top:*** Middle Anacapa Island. ***Bottom:*** Cathedral Cove.

Island morning glory threads itself through a coastal sagebrush.

Anacapa is dwarfed by nearby Santa Cruz Island, as seen in this view from Pt. Mugu.

CHAPTER TWO

Santa Cruz Island

Mysterious sea caves, steep cliffs, and white sandy beaches beckon the visitor to Santa Cruz Island—at 96 square miles, the largest of the Channel Islands. Santa Cruz's sheer bulk gives it the feel of a miniature continent. The rugged 77-mile coastline recalls how Southern California's mainland coast must have looked prior to development.

One of the island's unique features is its central valley bordered by two mountainous ridges, visible evidence of the Santa Cruz Island fault. Two distinct land masses—one volcanic, and one sedimentary in origin—come together at this point. The Channel Islands' highest mountain, Picacho Diablo, tops 2,400 feet.

According to Chumash legend, Santa Cruz Island was once connected to the mainland 19 miles away by a rainbow bridge. Island Chumash named Santa Cruz *Limuw,* "in the sea," while Mainland Chumash called it *Michumash,* "place of the islanders." Spanish explorers found upwards of 2,000 inhabitants in at least a dozen villages. During the Portolá expedition of 1769, a Franciscan priest lost his staff topped with an iron cross. The Chumash returned it the next day, giving rise to the name *Isla de la Santa Cruz* ("Island of the Holy Cross").

By 1807 a measles epidemic wiped out much of the Chumash population. The survivors were removed to the mainland shortly thereafter. In 1839 the Mexican governor granted ownership of Santa Cruz to Andres Castillero, and the Santa Cruz Island ranch became one of the most successful sheep operations in California.

In 1869 ownership passed to a group of 10 investors from San Francisco. One of these men, Justinian Caire, ultimately acquired all stock in the corporation and spearheaded a prosperous ranch, which raised sheep, Durham cattle, hay, and alfalfa. Over 200 acres were planted to wine grapes, and two large brick buildings housed the Santa Cruz Island winery. These buildings, as well as the chapel and other ranch structures, are still used today by The Nature Conservancy and the Santa Cruz Island Foundation.

The eastern portion of Santa Cruz Island is owned by the National Park Service and is open to the public. The remainder is controlled by The Nature Conservancy, and can be visited through naturalist-led day trips and special excursions.

Excellent boat anchorages surround the island. Some of the more popular landing spots for visitors are Scorpion Ranch, Smugglers Cove, and Prisoners' Harbor. The only marked hiking trail leads from Prisoners' Harbor to Pelican Bay, where visitors can see the remains of a resort that flourished in the early 1900s. A number of silent movies were filmed here, among them *Heart of My Heart* (1912), *Male and Female* (1919), and *Peter Pan* (1924).

Biologists prize the habitat of Santa Cruz Island as the most diverse in the Channel Islands. Endemic plants include island lace pod, island manzanita, silver lotus, island mallow, gooseberry, and monkey flower. The Santa Cruz Island jay is 25 percent larger and also bluer than its mainland counterpart. Four native terrestrial mammals dwell here: the tiny island fox, spotted skunk, deer mouse, and western harvest mouse.

On the northwest side of Santa Cruz Island, wind, wave, and faulting action have created California's largest sea cave in a steep volcanic cliff. Known as Painted Cave for its colorful lichens, algae, and mineral deposits, this natural phenomenon is inhabited by sea lions, harbor seals, and marine birds. Painted Cave and other sea caves are popular with kayakers who come to explore the island's many-faceted shoreline.

Opposite: Smuggler's Cove.

Top: Smuggler's Cove, sunrise.
Bottom: San Pedro Canyon.

Top: Goldfields, San Pedro Point.
Bottom: Smuggler's Cove, moonrise.

A lone oak tree on North Ridge, above Santa Cruz's Central Valley.

Top: Santa Cruz Island fox. ***Bottom:*** Santa Cruz Island silver lotus.
Both are endemic to the island.

Diverse flora is found in many of the steep, rugged canyons of Santa Cruz Island,
such as here in Smuggler's Canyon.

Santa Cruz Island wildflowers.
Left to right: Golden yarrow, snow berry, island bush poppy.

View from above Willows Anchorage looking west toward Santa Rosa Island.

Striking floral displays color Fraser Point, the
westernmost part of Santa Cruz Island.

Top: Goldfields and checker bloom.
Bottom: Checker bloom detail.

La Cascada is popular during the warm summer
months as a cooling-off spot.

This footbridge joins two sections of the historic Christy's Ranch.

Many of the Main Ranch buildings were built with island-made brick.
Left to right: Dairy, built in 1888; stable, completed in 1888; chapel, built in 1891.

46

The historic Main Ranch, nestled in the Central Valley.

CHAPTER THREE

Santa Rosa Island

The second largest of the Channel Islands, Santa Rosa Island stretches 15 miles long by 10 miles wide. Its terrain varies from broad, grass-covered slopes to mountains with deeply etched canyons. The Chumash called this island *Wimal,* translated as "driftwood." Many settled here, drawn by plentiful food and clear, freshwater springs and streams; to date, over 600 archeological sites have been identified.

Even earlier, Santa Rosa was home to prehistoric mammoths. More mammoth fossils have been uncovered here than on any other Channel Island. In 1994 archeologists excavated the most complete skeleton ever found of a rare pygmy mammoth, dating back 12,000 years. The rich Pleistocene fossil beds on the northern end of the island reveal the presence of other creatures such as giant mice, flightless geese, and vampire bats.

The severe earthquake of 1812, which destroyed the Santa Barbara Mission on the mainland, had its epicenter close to Santa Rosa Island. A massive rift opened on the island near Lobos Canyon—1,000 feet long, 100 feet wide, and 50 feet deep. This incident may have caused the remaining Chumash to depart for the mainland.

In the 1840s and 1850s, the days of old Spanish California, the island was a cattle rancheria. Subsequently the More family took over and built a thriving sheep ranch. In 1902 the island was purchased by Vail & Vickers, and cattle were reintroduced.

Vail & Vickers maintained private ownership of Santa Rosa Island from 1902 to 1986, at which time the U.S. government purchased the island and added it to Channel Islands National Park. Under a special use permit, Vail & Vickers ran cattle from the main ranch at Becher's Bay until 1998. Mexican *vaqueros* conducted round-ups every year, often fashioning their own rope, saddles, and bridles. A floating cattle pen, the 65-foot, wooden-hulled *Vaquero II,* transported the cattle to and from the mainland.

Not far from the main ranch, a stand of Torrey pines grows at elevations of 200-500 feet—the only native Torrey pines on the Channel Islands. Bishop pine forests can be found at slightly higher altitudes. Twelve groves of endemic island oaks dot the grassy hillsides. Visitors may come upon elk and deer, which were introduced to Santa Rosa as game animals in the early 1900s and are still hunted today. Less visible are the native mammals, including the endemic spotted skunk and subspecies of both deer mouse and island fox.

Santa Rosa Island's coastline encompasses marine terraces with steep cliffs and isolated, sandy beaches. Harbor seals, elephant seals, and sea lions haul out along the shore. On the island's eastern end, a unique coastal marsh forms the most extensive freshwater habitat on the Channel Islands. Together, the island's grasslands and marshlands support over 195 species of land and marine birds, from European starlings to Brandt's cormorants.

Just offshore, numerous shipwrecks surround Santa Rosa Island, one of the most recent being the *Chickasaw* in 1962. This freighter, en route from Japan with a cargo of toys and optical supplies, ran aground on the south side of the island; large pieces of its broken hull remain exposed today. Other favorite spots on Santa Rosa are the four-mile stretch of pristine beach near the campground at Water Canyon; the spectacular beach and sea caves at Southeast Anchorage; and the unique sculptured sandstone formations at Lobos Canyon.

Opposite: Torrey Pine, Bechers Bay.

Cattle and horses graze near the freshwater marsh on the east end of the island.

Cattle are transported to and from the island aboard the *Vaquero II*.

Evening settles over Skunk Point, with Santa Cruz Island in the distance.

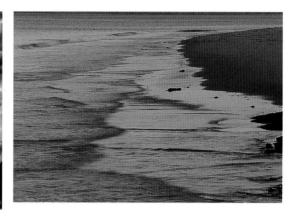

Left: The remains of the *Jane L. Stanford,* wrecked in 1929, lie at Southeast Anchorage.
Center: Munchkin dudleya, a plant endemic to East Point.
Right: Sunset color on the wide, sandy beaches of Skunk Point.

Sunrise illumines the rocky landscape of East Point.

Wind and water erosion have carved the sandstone walls of Lobos Canyon.

Skunk Point is home to a diverse community of birds.

Birds commonly found on Skunk Point.
Clockwise from top left: Sanderling; black oystercatcher; long-billed curlew,
black-bellied plover, whimbrel; snowy plover.

Top: Severe erosion has created a stark landscape around these island oak trees.
Bottom: Erosion has exposed the roots of this island oak.
Opposite: A year-round stream flows through Acapulco Canyon.

Opposite: Lace lichen shrouds the limbs of a dead tree on Black Mountain.
Above, left to right: Island monkey flower,
Greene's live-forever, common monkey flower.

Previous pages: Sunset at Johnsons Lee on Santa Rosa's south side.
Above: Historic ranch buildings, built in the late 1800's.

The tack room at the ranch is still in use today.

CHAPTER FOUR

San Miguel Island

Windswept and remote, San Miguel Island is a sanctuary of outstanding natural beauty. The third largest island in the park, with a total area of 14 square miles, it consists of a gently sloping plateau—in contrast to the more rugged terrain of other Channel Islands. Two rounded hills emerge from this plateau, San Miguel Peak and Green Mountain.

As the westernmost of the Northern Channel Islands, San Miguel Island often experiences severe weather. Strong northwest winds, fog, and cool temperatures are the norm. Submerged rocks and shoals make the surrounding waters hazardous for sailors, who know San Miguel as "the graveyard of the Pacific" because of the shipwrecks that have occurred here.

The Chumash called this island *Tuqan,* a name that has no known translation. Radiocarbon dating indicates that Native Americans inhabited San Miguel over 10,700 years ago. Archaeologists conducted extensive excavations in the late nineteenth and twentieth centuries, and to date over 600 archaeological sites have been identified on the island.

In 1542, explorer Juan Rodríguez Cabrillo became the first European to land on San Miguel Island. According to legend, it may be his final resting place. Cabrillo sustained injuries when he fell out of his skiff while coming ashore, and died of a subsequent infection in the winter of 1543. Though his grave was never found, a monument honoring him was placed above Cuyler Harbor in 1937.

Ranchers raised sheep and some cattle on the island from 1850 to 1948. George Nidever was the first to begin ranching in earnest when he moved to the island in 1852. Two other prominent individuals from this period are Captain William G. Waters, who conducted wool-growing operations from 1887 to 1917; and Robert Brooks, who held grazing leases from 1917 to 1948. Between 1930-1942 Herbert Lester—a colorful character known as "The King of San Miguel"—managed the island for Brooks.

During the 1950s and 1960s San Miguel Island was used as a bombing range by the U.S. Navy. Today San Miguel and its smaller neighbor, Prince Island, are still owned by the Navy and managed by the National Park Service.

Because the island's plant and animal communities were extensively damaged by grazing, all feral sheep and burros were removed by the late 1970s. Since then, native plant communities have made a comeback, stabilizing the soil and sand from the strong winds. Over 200 plant species include flowering varieties such as coreopsis and lupine, plus a variety of native and introduced grasses.

Two of the fascinating natural attractions that draw visitors to San Miguel Island are Point Bennett, a breeding ground for pinnipeds; and the island's spectacular Caliche Forest. Huge colonies of seals and sea lions arrive every year at Point Bennett in one of the world's outstanding wildlife displays. Six species have been known to use this sandy peninsula as a breeding ground or resting place—California sea lion, Steller sea lion, northern fur seal, Guadalupe fur seal, northern elephant seal, and harbor seal. Up to 10,000 animals may be found on the beach at one time in the spring. All except the Steller sea lion and Guadalupe fur seal are common and breed here.

Inland, sand and wind have exposed the Caliche Forest. The calcified remains of large tree trunks provide evidence that the island once supported an ancient forest. The plants' organic acids reacted with calcium carbonate to form the ghostly pillars, a chemical transformation that took thousands of years to complete. This is the most extensive caliche deposit in the Channel Islands.

Opposite: Caliche Forest.

This monument honoring explorer Juan Rodríguez Cabrillo
was placed above Cuyler Harbor in 1937.

The remains of a fence stand as a reminder of the island's ranching history.

Summer-blooming red buckwheat follows spring displays of
giant coreopsis in Nidever Canyon.

Greene's live-forever assumes a variety of shapes and colors along
Harris Point Trail.

The sculpting power of wind at work in Cuyler Harbor.
Left: A spectacular example of caliche. *Above:* Sand dunes.

Left: One of the world's finest displays of pinnipeds can be seen at Point Bennett.
Above: Northern elephant seals.

A magnificent floral display along Harris Point Trail.

Clockwise from upper left: California poppy, San Luis Obispo locoweed,
succulent lupine, San Miguel Island locoweed.

Fog descends over the turquoise waters and sandy beaches of Cuyler Harbor.

Midden sites, like this one near Cuyler Harbor, reveal that the Chumash occupied
San Miguel for over 10,000 years.

Brightened by the red indian paintbrush, Nidever Canyon is the only access
to the island from Cuyler Harbor.
Opposite: Summer-blooming red buckwheat provides the primary color accent in August.

Low lying clouds and fog often obscure the upper elevations of the trail to Point Bennett.

Blue-eyed grass is interspersed throughout the meadows along the trail to Point Bennett.

Cuyler Point with Prince Island in the background.

San Miguel Island wildflowers.
Left to right: Yarrow, purple owl's clover, seaside daisy.

CHAPTER FIVE

Santa Barbara Island

At 38 miles offshore, and just one square mile in area, Santa Barbara Island appears at first to be little more than a barren rock. Yet once ashore, visitors notice that the calling of gulls and the barking of sea lions can be heard from one end of the island to the other. Next, the rich intertidal zone and the diversity of plants on the surface become apparent. Soon it is clear that, like the other Channel Islands, Santa Barbara Island teems with plant, bird, and animal life.

The only member of the Southern Channel Islands to be included in the park, Santa Barbara Island is visible from few mainland vantage points. On all sides, steep cliffs rise to a triangular-shaped marine terrace whose highest point is Signal Peak (635 feet). Shortages of fuel and water prevented the Gabrieliño people of the Southern Channel Islands from establishing permanent settlements here; however, they used it as a resting place during inter-island journeys.

Santa Barbara Island was named by the European explorer Sebastian Vizcaíno, who put ashore on Saint Barbara's Day, December 4, 1602. A few squatters—fishermen, seal hunters, and Chinese lobster trappers— resided here in the late nineteenth century. H. Bay Webster, a lessee of Anacapa Island, built a cabin on Santa Barbara Island at the point that now bears his name.

After U.S. government leasing took effect at the turn of the century, the island's most noteworthy residents were the Hyder family, who raised sheep from 1914-1922. Ranching took its toll on the island's native vegetation, a problem compounded by the introduction of New Zealand red rabbits in the 1940s—a time when the island was used by the U.S. Navy as an early

SHAG ROCK

Arch Point

Webster Point

Elephant Seal Cove

Landing Cove

North Peak 562 ft.

Cave Canyon

Signal Peak 635 ft.

Sea Lion Rookery

NORTH

SUTIL ISLAND

Cat Canyon

warning outpost. The National Park Service eliminated the rabbits in 1984, and now the recovering landscape provides renewed habitat for nesting birds, night lizards, the island deer mouse, and six species of land mollusks.

Santa Barbara Island provides a superb habitat for birds. Nearly 70 species have been observed, including three species of cormorants, Cassin's auklets, and Xantus' murrelets. Despite its small size, the island is the second most important of the Channel Islands for nesting seabirds. There is a large western gull rookery, and endangered California brown pelicans have nested on the island since 1980. The population of Xantus' murrelets numbers in the thousands, and is believed to be the largest breeding colony of that species in the world. These birds create their nests by burrowing into the steep hillsides and cliffs; within 48 hours after hatching the chicks plunge into the ocean, where they spend the rest of their lives before returning to the island to breed.

Visitors to Santa Barbara Island disembark at Landing Cove and hike up 160 steps to the top of the mesa. Approximately 5.5 miles of trails make the island's attractions easily accessible on foot. From the cliff overlooking Elephant Seal Cove, visitors can observe sea lion pups being born in early summer, or elephant seals breeding in the winter months. At Webster Point, the trail leads past the gull rookery, where chicks hatch in late May and early June.

Santa Barbara Island experiences a more temperate climate than that of the four northern Channel Islands, with daytime temperatures ranging from 50 to 80 degrees. On a clear day, every member of the Channel Islands chain is visible from Santa Barbara Island—with the exception of San Miguel Island, which is blocked from view by its larger neighbor, Santa Rosa Island.

Opposite: Signal Peak.

The smallest of the Channel Islands, Santa Barbara Island is one square mile in size.

Clockwise from upper left:
Coralline algae and brown algae, rock daisy, coastal cholla, blue dick.

A California sea lion and her pup basking in the sun at Elephant Seal Cove.

In late spring and early summer, California sea lions aggressively protect their newborn pups from
the much larger Northern elephant seals.

Opposite and above: Introduced grains and grasses, such as Mediterranean
canary grass, compete vigorously with native plants.

Evening light falls across Webster Point,
the westernmost tip of Santa Barbara Island.

A colorful display of blue dicks near the base of Signal Peak.
In the distance is Sutil Island.

Low tides reveal agar weed, an ochre starfish, and other marine life
in a small sea cave near Landing Cove.

The rugged shoreline near Landing Cove is bathed in soft pre-dawn light.

Commercial fisherman and recreational boaters
find refuge in the quiet waters of Landing Cove.

Normally covered by high tides, the intertidal zone on the east side of the island consists
of a narrow, steeply sloping shore backed by precipitous cliffs.

One of the largest western gull rookeries in the
Channel Islands is located at Webster Point.

Western gulls usually lay two or three eggs per nest.
Parents take turns nest-sitting.

Elephant Seal Cove Trail traverses the grass-covered slopes of the island.

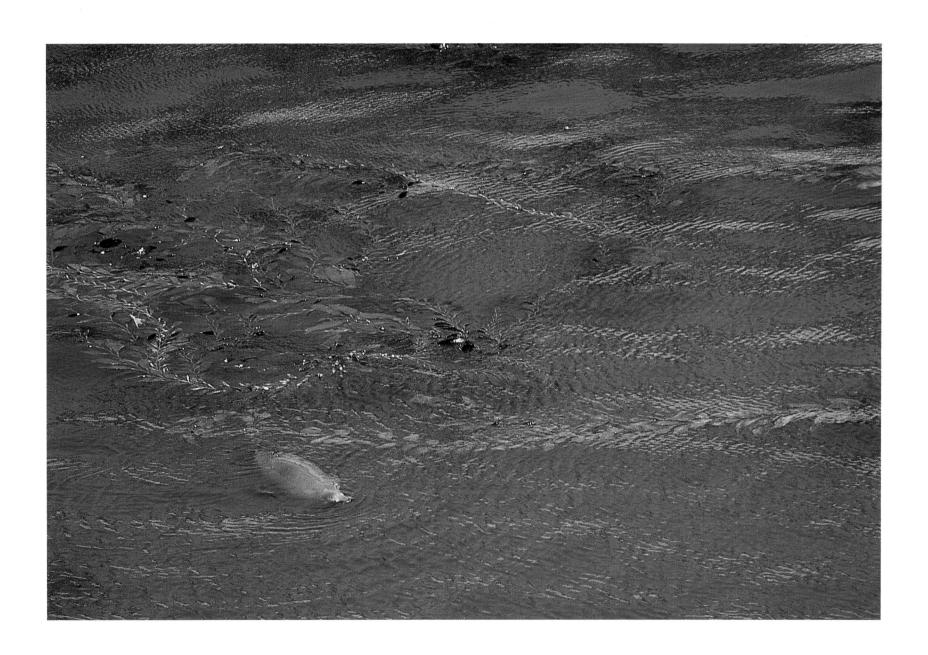

A Northern elephant seal swims about in the clear, kaleidoscopic waters of Elephant Seal Cove.

Spring rains transform the slopes of North Peak into a garden paradise.
Top: Giant coreopsis. ***Bottom:*** Santa Barbara Island cream cups.

A spectacular display of giant coreopsis dominates this view
of Arch Point from Canyon View Nature Trail.

The silver-gray foliage of Trask's locoweed is conspicuous on the rocky coastal
slopes between North Peak and Arch Point.

Left to right: Silver lotus, Santa Barbara Island live-forever,
dormant giant coreopsis.

A sunset view of Sutil Island, a rocky outcropping off the
southwest coast of Santa Barbara Island.

An early June sunrise across North Peak.

Appendix

TERRESTRIAL PLANTS

Bishop Pine *(Pinus muricata)*
Blue Dick *(Dichelostemma capitatum)*
Blue-eyed Grass *(Sisyrinchium bellum)*
California Poppy *(Eschscholzia californica)*
Candleholder Dudleya *(Dudleya candelabrum)*
Checker Bloom *(Sidalcea malviflora)*
Coastal Sagebrush *(Artemisia californica)*
Coastal Cholla *(Opuntia prolifera)*
Common Monkey Flower *(Mimulus guttatus)*
Giant Coreopsis *(Coreopsis gigantea)*
Golden Yarrow *(Eriophyllum confertiflorum)*
Goldfields *(Lasthenia californica)*
Greene's Live-forever *(Dudleya greenei)*
Indian Paint Brush *(Castilleja affinis)*
Island Bush Poppy *(Dendromecon rigida*
  subsp. *harfordii)* (1)
Island Cherry *(Prunus ilicifolia* subsp. *lyonii)*
Island Manzanita *(Arctostaphylos tomentosa*
  subsp. *insulicola)*
Island Monkey Flower *(Mimulus flemingii)*
Island Morning Glory *(Calystegia macrostegia*
  subsp. *macrostegia)*
Island Oak *(Quercus tomentella)*
Island Torrey Pine *(Pinus torreyana* subsp. *insularis)* (2)
Mediterranean Canary Grass *(Phalaris minor)*
McMinn's Manzanita *(Arctostaphylos viridissima)* (1)
Munchkin Dudleya *(Dudleya gnoma)* (2)
Purple Owl's Clover *(Castilleja exserta)*
Rancheria Clover *(Trifolium albopurpureum)*
Red Buckwheat *(Eriogonum grande* var. *rubescens)*
Rock Daisy *(Perityle emoryi)*
San Miguel Island Locoweed *(Astragalus miguelensis)*
San Luis Obispo Locoweed *(Astragalus curtipes)*
Santa Barbara Island Cream Cups *(Platystemon*
  californicus var. *ciliatus)* (3)
Santa Barbara Island Live-forever *(Dudleya traskiae)* (3)
Santa Cruz Island Gooseberry *(Ribes thacherianum)* (1)
Santa Cruz Island Ironwood *(Lyonothamnus floribundus*
  subsp. *aspleniifolius)*
Santa Cruz Island Lace Pod *(Thysanocarpus*
  conchuliferus) (1)
Santa Cruz Island Mallow *(Malaconthamnus fasciculatus*
  var. *nesioticus)* (1)
Santa Cruz Island Manzanita *(Arctostaphylos insularis)* (1)
Santa Cruz Island Monkey Flower *(Mimulus*
  brandegeei) (1)
Santa Cruz Island Silver Lotus *(Lotus argophyllus*
  var. *niveus)* (1)
Sea Rocket *(Cakile maritima)*
Seaside Daisy *(Erigeron glaucus)*
Silver Lotus *(Lotus argophyllus* var. *ornithopus)*
Snow Berry *(Symphoricarpos mollis)*
Subcordate Manzanita *(Arctostaphylos tomentosa*
  subsp. *subcordata)*
Succulent Lupine *(Lupinus succulentus)*
Trask's Locoweed *(Astragalus traskiae)*
Yarrow *(Achillea millefolium)*

MARINE PLANTS

Agar Weed *(Gelidium)*
Brown Algae *(Halidrys dioica)*
Coralline Algae *(Bossiella)* or *(Calliarthron)*
Giant Bladder Kelp *(Macrocystis pyrifera)*

LEGEND

(E) Endangered; **(T)** Threatened; **(1)** Endemic to Santa
Cruz Island; **(2)** Endemic to Santa Rosa Island;
(3) Endemic to Santa Barbara Island;
(4) Endemic to San Miguel Island.

*This appendix is a scientific listing of the plants and animals
shown or refered to in this book. It is not intended as a complete listing of all the plants and animals that can be found
on and around the Channel Islands.*

Opposite: Anacapa Island.

BIRDS

Black Oystercatcher *(Haematopus bachmani)*
Brandt's Cormorant *(Phalacrocorax penicillatus)*
California Brown Pelican *(Pelecanus occidentalis)* (E)
Cassin's Auklet *(Ptychoramphus aleuticus)*
European Starling *(Sturnus vulgaris)*
Long-billed Curlew *(Numenius americanus)*
Pigeon Guillemot *(Cepphus columba)*
Sanderling *(Calidris alba)*
Santa Cruz Island Jay *(Aphelocoma coerulescens*
  insularis) (1)
Snowy Plover *(Charadrius alexandrinus)* (T)
Western Gull *(Larus occidentalis)*
Whimbrel *(Numenius phaeopus)*
Xantus Murrelet *(Synthliboramphus hypoleucus)*

TERRESTRIAL ANIMALS

Deer Mouse *(Peromyscus maniculatus)*
Island Night Lizard *(Xantusia riversiana)* (T)
Santa Cruz Island Fox *(Urocyon littoralis santacruzae)*
  (1)(T)
San Miguel Island Fox *(Urocyon littoralis littoralis)*
  (4)(T)
Santa Rosa Island Fox *(Urocyon littoralis santarosae)*
  (2)(T)
Spotted Skunk *(Spilogale gracilis amphiala)*
Western Harvest Mouse *(Reithrodontomys megalotis)*

MARINE ANIMALS

California Sea Lion *(Zalophus californianus)*
California Gray Whale *(Eschrichtius robustus)*
Green Sea Anemone *(Anthopleura elegantissima)*
Guadalupe Fur Seal *(Arctocephalus townsendi)* (T)
Harbor Seal *(Phoca vitulina)*
Northern Fur Seal *(Callorhinus ursinus)*
Northern Elephant Seal *(Mirounga angustirostris)*
Ochre Starfish *(Pisaster ochraceus)*
Stellar Sea Lion *(Eumetopias jubatus)* (T)